20TH CENTURY *fashion*

THE 70s

PUNKS, GLAM ROCKERS, & NEW ROMANTICS

For a free color catalog describing Gareth Stevens Publishing's list of high-quality books
and multimedia programs, call 1-800-542-2595 (USA) or 1-800-461-9120 (Canada).
Gareth Stevens Publishing's Fax: (414) 225-0377.

Library of Congress Cataloging-in-Publication Data available upon request from publisher.
Fax: (414) 225-0377 for the attention of the Publishing Records Department.

ISBN 0-8368-2602-7

This North American edition first published in 2000 by
Gareth Stevens Publishing
1555 North RiverCenter Drive, Suite 201
Milwaukee, Wisconsin 53212 USA

Original edition © 1999 by David West Children's Books. First published in Great Britain in 1999
by Heinemann Library, Halley Court, Jordan Hill, Oxford OX2 8EJ, a division of Reed Educational
and Professional Publishing Limited. This U.S. edition © 2000 by Gareth Stevens, Inc. Additional
end matter © 2000 by Gareth Stevens, Inc.

Editor: Clare Oliver
Picture Research: Carlotta Cooper/Brooks Krikler Research
Consultant: Helen Reynolds

Gareth Stevens Series Editor: Dorothy L. Gibbs

Photo Credits:
Abbreviations: (t) top, (m) middle, (b) bottom, (l) left, (r) right

BBC Picture Archive: page 18(tl)
Hulton Getty: pages 4(br), 5(tr, br, bl), 10-11, 12(bl), 12-13, 19(br), 20(bl), 21(tl), 22(tl), 28(bl, br)
Kobal Collection: pages 7(tr), 13(tl), 19(tr)
Redferns: Cover (ml), pages 3(ml), 4-5, 10(tl), 11(br), 16(tl), 18(bl), 20(r), 20-21, 22(bl, r), 23(l),
24(bl), 24-25, 25(br)
Frank Spooner Pictures: Cover (tl), pages 3(tl), 14(r), 15(mr), 16-17
© *Vogue*/Condé Nast Publications Ltd: / Clive Arrowsmith: Cover (bm), pages 8(br), 26(tl), 26-27,
27(tr) / Eric Boman: pages 17(bc), 24(tl) / Alex Chatelain: pages 10(bl), 12(tl), 14(ml, mr), 15(tl),
18-19, 21(tr, br) / Willie Christie: Cover (br), pages 15(br), 25(tr), 26(bl) / Henry Clarke: page 6(br) /
Arthur Elgort: pages 7(br), 28(tl), 29(rm) / Jonvelle: pages 6-7 / Peter Knapp: page 9(bl) /
Barry Lategan: Cover (bl2), pages 8(bl), 11(tr), 13(br) / Sarah Moon: page 6(tl) / Lothar Schmid:
Cover (br), pages 3(mr), 9(m), 18(r), 23(mr), 29(bl) / Carolyn Shultz: page 9(tl) / Albert Watson:
Cover (bl1), pages 16(bl), 17(mr)

With special thanks to the Picture Library and Syndication Department at *Vogue* Magazine/Condé
Nast Publications Ltd.

Printed in Mexico

1 2 3 4 5 6 7 8 9 04 03 02 01 00

20TH CENTURY
fashion
THE '70s

PUNKS, GLAM ROCKERS, & NEW ROMANTICS

Sarah Gilmour

Gareth Stevens Publishing
MILWAUKEE

Contents

Shorter-than-short, tight-fitting hot pants reinvented the mini.

The Glam and Glossy 1970s

This protester is wearing a gas mask in a demonstration against nuclear weapons (1971).

Disco and glam crazes created a fashion for all that glistened.

Glamorous, frivolous, and more than slightly ridiculous, platforms and flares or bell-bottoms now epitomize, to many people, "the decade that style forgot." There was, however, more to the 1970s than extreme fashion. It was a turbulent, often violent, decade. The Vietnam War continued, and wars raged in the Middle East. The oil crisis contributed to recession and rising unemployment in the West, and political scandals provoked even greater unrest.

With marches and demonstrations, marginalized groups, including blacks, women, and gays, fought for the right to be equal. Protests often took a violent turn. Certain political groups even resorted to guerrilla tactics, such as hijackings and letter bombs, to get their voices heard.

Hippie ideals of peace and love were abandoned in favor of personal gain. Health and fitness became a craze. People looked for ways to escape through the nostalgia or fantasy of film and fashion.

Fashion reflected many of the decade's changes and obsessions. Army surplus and retro styles became popular. It was a decade characterized by extremes, an informal approach to dressing, and a greater choice of styles.

The United States was shaken by the Watergate scandal, and, in 1974, President Richard M. Nixon made history as the first U.S. president to resign from office. Burglars connected with officials in Nixon's government were caught in the opposition party's headquarters.

Outrageous fashions of the 1970s included ankle-breaking platform shoes.

Retro Dressing

In search of romance, some designers harked back to art deco. Soft, feminine colors included moss green and aubergine.

Many people who had aspired to peace and love in the 1960s became disillusioned in the 1970s with wars, unemployment, and social inequality. Fashion turned to the past to escape the present.

DROPPING OUT

Aging hippies used clothing to express their disgust with the commercial Western world. Since the fashion industry was a part of this consumer society, hippies bought clothes from secondhand and vintage clothing stores or made their own clothes. Lace blouses, long skirts, and buttoned boots were mixed with ethnic shawls and handmade sweaters.

RETRO ROMANCE

Designers were quick to pick up on hippie styles. Bill Gibb (1943–1988) mixed Celtic and historical references. Zandra Rhodes (*b.* 1940) based her 1970 collections on Ukrainian shawls and American Indian clothing. Ossie Clark (1942–1996) led the revival for high-necked, Edwardian blouses teamed with floor-length skirts. Laura Ashley (1925–1985), who opened her first shop in 1967, popularized the milkmaid look with feminine and delicate flowery fabrics based on country prints.

A sheer blouse and a silk patchwork skirt created an ethnic Eastern look.

HOLLYWOOD GLAMOUR

Historical influences also created a darker, more glamorous retro-chic as fashions of the 1920s, 1930s, and, particularly, the 1940s were revisited. Secondhand shops were raided, again — this time for little dresses in "trashy" fabrics such as rayon. Teamed with platform shoes and faux fur coats, outfits recreated the images of 1940s film stars.

Bold, sporting checks were based on the country-casual look of men in the 1920s.

ART DECO

The fashion for 1930's art deco was epitomized by Biba, the shop owned by Barbara Hulanicki (*b.* 1936). In 1973, Biba moved into an old building with an art deco interior. In 1972, Karl Lagerfeld (*b.* 1938) produced a deco collection for the French ready-to-wear label *Chloé*.

PERSONAL TASTE

In the 1970s, fashion was no longer strictly followed as it changed each season. Individuality and personal taste became more important. People could avoid the main-stream and wear styles that set them apart from the crowd.

The American film Bonnie and Clyde *(1967), starring Faye Dunaway and Warren Beatty, popularized the 1930s style.*

RETRO MOVIES

Bonnie and Clyde was as much about attitude as it was about fashion. Bank robbers on the run, Clyde wore a double-breasted suit, and Bonnie wore a knee-length, A-line skirt and a beret, a look soon to be copied on catwalks and on the street. Other films that inspired retro fashions were *The Boyfriend* (1971), starring model Twiggy as a 1920s flapper, and *Cabaret* (1972), set in 1930s Berlin and starring Liza Minnelli.

Pants called Oxford bags were worn by men in the 1920s and by women in the 1930s. In the 1970s, they were the alternative to flares.

The Mystic Orient

From the hippies at the opening of the decade to the new romantics at its close, the influence of the East on Western fashion was a recurring theme in the 1970s.

WEST GOES EAST

Why the fascination with the East? During the 1970s, the Middle East was rarely out of the headlines. The Yom Kippur War of 1973 and the subsequent rise in oil prices by seventy percent caused a global crisis. The extraordinary artifacts from the tomb of eighteenth-century pharaoh Tutankhamen in Egypt, which were exhibited at the British Museum in 1972, brought on a craze for all things Egyptian. Less expensive air travel enabled more people to take vacations to the Orient and other exotic locations. Even health and fitness were affected by popular interest in the Eastern exercises of yoga and t'ai chi.

PICK AND MIX

Although Eastern influences on fashion were not just a phenomenon of the 1970s, they fit in extremely well with the popular themes of that decade: fantasy, glamour, escapism, nostalgia, and the quest for novelty. Designers transformed traditional costumes into fashionable garments, then moved on to something new.

This stunning turban was an exotic accessory that brought a sense of mystique and romance to Western fashion.

ZANDRA RHODES

More than any other designer in the 1970s, Zandra Rhodes was influenced by various cultures and countries, from Mexico to Australia. In 1979, she visited China, where she was inspired by the heavy makeup and headdresses worn in Chinese opera. She also decorated her fabrics with circular designs based on the stone carvings of water and clouds in ancient Chinese palaces. Some of her designs even reflected Chinese architecture — one blouse had pagoda sleeves. Rhodes also drew heavily on Chinese clothing itself, employing traditions such as quilting.

The taste for the exotic could also be seen in a colonial style, such as this cool linen shirt and trousers with a panama hat.

Fashion items from the East were recreated in ultramodern materials. This coolie hat (1977) was made of blue PVC material.

ASIA AND THE PACIFIC

Turbans were revived as part of the retro-chic look, and sarongs were adopted as beachwear. Turkish harem pants and the caftan, a loose, ankle-length robe that originated in ancient Mesopotamia, became popular evening wear. All these items appeared in modern fabrics and cuts to give them a Western flavor.

GYPSY CHIC

Eastern Europe seemed just as exotic as the Far East. The gypsy look, with its flounced skirts, low necklines, and colorful sashes and scarfs, was exploited by designers Caroline Charles (*b*. 1942) and Thea Porter (*b*. 1927).

COSSACK COUTURE

Yves Saint Laurent (*b*. 1936) turned to Russia for inspiration. In 1976, he sent his models down the catwalk in baggy trousers tucked into cossack boots, full-flowing dresses, and fur hats. Decoration on these items included braiding, embroidery, and brocade. Pure fairy tale, these clothes were far beyond the means of the average woman.

This rice-paddy look of 1973 by designer Kenzo was for his own shop.

Glam and Glitter

In a decade of outrageous fashions, "glam" was the most outrageous, by far. Platform shoes, padded shoulders, flared pants, and synthetic fabrics were adopted by serious and not-so-serious rock stars and worn as spectacular stage costumes.

Marc Bolan, lead singer of T Rex, wore glittery suits and fashionably long hair.

FACTORY MADE

In the 1960s and 1970s, pop artist Andy Warhol (1928–1987) and followers at his studio, the Factory, were a huge influence on art, film, and fashion. Film star Candy Darling and performance band The Exploding Plastic Inevitable set the tone for gender ambiguity and dressing up, which were key elements of glam style.

GLAM ROCKERS

Glam rock spawned a new generation of superstars whose appeal depended as much on their looks and their image as their music. Performers, such as the New York Dolls, Alice Cooper, T Rex, and David Bowie, strutted the stage in face paint and feather boas. Platform shoes got higher, flares got wider, and hair got longer. Satin, velvet, and suede were the favorite fabrics — all liberally sprinkled with sequins. Makeup was essential, and both the guys and the girls wore eyeliner and glitter eyeshadow.

Calvin Klein's bronze suede jacket and gold gauze trousers (1979) demonstrate over-the-top glamour.

THE IMPACT OF GLAM

Such wild attire really was not meant for daily wear — tall platform boots made it pretty hard to run for a bus! You needed only to look at the audiences on television music shows to see the difference between stagewear and streetwear. In 1972, while Alice Cooper sang "School's Out" wearing leather flares and runny mascara, his school-age fans wore frilly dresses or tank tops. Equivalents of glam outfits, however, could be found at shops such as Paraphernalia in New York and Mr. Freedom in London.

CHANGING IDEAS

Without the permissiveness that began in the 1960s, glam would never have existed. The attitude effected by glam rockers made the idea of alternate lifestyles less of a taboo — even though most of the glam musicians themselves probably led more traditional lifestyles.

FANTASY WORLD

Glam fashion delighted in the extreme, the tacky, and the shocking. Because it was mainly confined to the stage, glam fashion was more about fantasy and escapism than it was a serious attempt to change anything in society.

High-fashion designers, including Kansai Yamamoto, borrowed elements of glam, such as these high-rise boots.

SPACE ODDITY

With his dyed hair, makeup, and earrings, David Bowie paraded costumes that included sequined leotards and thigh-high platform boots. His androgynous look, with both masculine and feminine qualities, shocked the older generation but inspired the young to question traditional roles.

In the 1970s, David Bowie reinvented himself as Ziggy Stardust and Aladdin Sane.

In the early 1970s, hot pants — short shorts in satin or suede — replaced the miniskirt.

Everyday Fashion

Not everyone enjoyed the glam and retro fashions. By 1973, the novelty was already wearing thin. Mainstream fashion avoided these extreme styles and began catering to the increasing demand for classic, wearable clothing.

HARD TIMES

Recession, high unemployment, and inflation in the early 1970s meant many people could not afford to spend much on fashion. Perhaps even those who could did not want to spend their money that way. So, for the first time, dressing down became more important than dressing up.

A crepe-de-chine A-line suit was perfect office attire in 1978.

THE OIL CRISIS

The Yom Kippur War, in 1973, between Israel and neighboring Arab countries led to cuts in oil deliveries to Western nations that were friendly to Israel. Rising oil prices and oil shortages resulted in inflation, recession, and unemployment. This crisis was reflected in the sober fashions of the period.

In 1973-1974, people tried to conserve energy in every way they possibly could.

THE END OF COUTURE?

With the fragmentation of fashion, the number of different styles to choose from, and the rise of alternative and anti-fashions, many people believed the 1970s would see the decline of haute couture. In response to changing attitudes, designers began to focus on classic clothes, producing prêt-à-porter, or ready-to-wear, collections that were more profitable than haute couture.

Men still wore suits to work, but the style was informal. Yves Saint Laurent's 1974 collection featured trousers with flared legs.

READY-TO-WEAR

Jean Muir (1933–1995), Sonia Rykiel (*b.* 1930), and Yves Saint Laurent were key figures in this fashion revolution. Muir and Rykiel were both renowned for their elegant garments in fluid jersey. Saint Laurent's trademark was the masculine tailored suit, known as a *smoking*. This style was adopted by newly liberated women who were fighting for recognition in the workplace. It was, however, American designers, such as Ralph Lauren (*b.* 1939) and Calvin Klein (*b.* 1942), who were best at designing relaxed ready-to-wear classics.

CAPSULE CHIC

Tweed jackets, knee-length skirts, slim-cut trousers, and smart sweaters and blouses became the basics of a working woman's wardrobe. Easily combined into a number of different looks, this "capsule" wardrobe has had a lasting effect on how women dress.

Stars of the TV hit "Charlie's Angels" wore fashionable hairstyles and oversized collars.

Another innovation, "seasonless dressing," meant fashion-conscious women did not have to change their look every season; they could wear the same pieces for several years, adding only coordinating items. The emphasis was on "cheap chic" as *Vogue* introduced its "More-Dash-Less-Cash" feature.

HEALTHY GOOD LOOKS

To complement the classic outfit, makeup was kept to a minimum in soft peaches and pinks for a natural look. Hair was shoulder length and off the face. Diet and exercise became obsessions to achieve good health and a slim figure.

Woody Allen's movie Annie Hall *promoted a look of effectively thrown-together separates.*

Physical Fashion

The 1970s saw a new craze for fitness. Designers such as Ralph Lauren, Yves Saint Laurent, and Calvin Klein produced figure-hugging fashions that required well-toned bodies.

LET'S GET PHYSICAL

To get their bodies in shape, men and women visited the gym and took up jogging, cycling, and even marathon running. Many people wanted specific types of clothing for these activities, but, initially, there was not a wide selection from which to choose.

Sportswear designers quickly began to recognize the rapidly expanding fitness market. Tracksuits and running shoes left the gym and hit the streets. Aerobics and dance classes helped popularize leotards and leg warmers.

Exercise attire had function and fashion, and it could double as dancewear and beachwear.

DESIGNER SPORTSWEAR

Betsey Johnson (*b.* 1942) brought out inspired bodysuits, leotards, and hot pants. Basic items, such as windbreakers and sweatshirts, were given a fashionable twist, using terry cloth and velour and cutting the fabric closer to the body.

Stylish designer Joseph created this practical cotton tracksuit featured in Vogue, *in summer 1979.*

WORK AND PLAY

Many women wanted to show off the bodies they worked so hard to achieve. In France, Sonia Rykiel popularized clinging, slinky knitwear. The United States specialized in body-conscious clothes. Many designers were influenced by Claire McCardell (1905–1958) who, in the 1940s, had taken simple fabrics, such as denim, to make what was known as "playwear."

GAME, SET, MATCH

The sports craze started with tennis. Players, such as Björn Borg and Chris Evert, were like rock stars. Slazenger, Head, and Adidas revamped tennis whites and added matching items, such as sweat bands. It was possible for the public to buy the same items as the tennis players.

Tennis star Chris Evert's dress bridged the gap between sports and fashion.

EASY STYLES

Physical fashion was all about feeling comfortable and looking relaxed. Men and women wanted stylish casual clothes, and, with less of a distinction between day and evening wear, sportswear provided an easy solution. Jazzed-up versions in silks, satins, or spandex also made perfect disco attire. Practical or showy sportswear offered an alternative to the extremes of fashion and taste that became the trademark of the 1970s.

Dance studios sold soft leather ballet slippers, leotards, and leg warmers.

Disco Dancing Queens

Discomania swept the United States and then Europe at the end of the 1970s. At clubs such as Studio 54 in New York, celebrities like Bianca Jagger, Calvin Klein, Elizabeth Taylor, and Andy Warhol were regulars. Discothèques created a fantasy world in which light shows dazzled, music thumped, and real life was left at the door.

*Disco favorites
The Jackson Five wore
glitzy outfits as standard
stagewear.*

WHAT TO WEAR?

With disco came glamour and a return to dressing up. On the crowded dance floor, eye-catching fashions were necessary to attract attention, and clothes had to look good under the powerful laser lights.

DISCO STYLE

Choosing what to wear added to the excitement — and what a choice there was! Almost anything went, but, since the main activities at a disco were dancing and posing, freedom to move was crucial.

*This Vogue model teamed a stretchy Lycra
bodysuit with a blue sequined jacket (1978).*

Playing Tony Manero in the 1977 movie Saturday Night Fever, *John Travolta boogied his way to fame.*

DISCO DESIGNERS

Many of the people at the most exclusive clubs were in the fashion business. Roy Halston (1932–1990) and Stephen Burrows (*b.* 1943) were kings of disco. For those who could afford his prices, Halston created halter-neck dresses and jumpsuits in jersey, chiffon, and Ultrasuede. Burrows was famous for his crinkled, "lettuce-leaf" hems and patchwork trousers. Most outrageous of all was the futuristic look, with body glitter and sequins, silver and gold lamé, or a Thierry Mugler jumpsuit. Not everyone, however, was so extreme!

ANYTHING GOES

For those on a budget, sportswear, such as satin running shorts teamed with a skimpy top, was an inexpensive option. A sequined evening dress, worn with cheap accessories, was also acceptable. Although it was completely at odds with the disco style, American preppie attire, consisting of jeans, a button-down shirt, and sneakers, was often seen on the dance floor, too.

DANCES WITH WHEELS

Roller disco developed its own brand of fashion. Companies, such as Danskin in the United States, produced leotards, bodysuits, and tights in brightly colored spandex with matching wraparound skirts. Stretchy spandex, the practical choice for this activity, was teamed with knee and elbow pads and a crash helmet.

Roller disco combined the crazes for both disco and roller skating.

Pearly green sequins and spike heels were alluring evening wear for a glamorous disco dancer.

Urban Warriors

A period of protest, the 1970s saw a number of groups campaigning for equal rights. Antiwar protests continued until the United States military withdrew from Vietnam in 1973.

Dressed in army surplus, Wolfie of the British television series "Citizen Smith" was an urban warrior.

MILITARY STYLES

Antiwar protesters dressed in army surplus, with combat pants, long hair, and a radical attitude, to parody a war they opposed. With U.S. troops on the nightly news and the success of *M*A*S*H*, the antiwar television series set in Korea, army surplus filtered into fashion.

LEATHER-CLAD

Some men, however, had a more flamboyant approach to fashion. Adopting macho styles and flaunting them openly, they confused the whole idea of masculinity. They wore not only army surplus, but also leather and work clothing, such as flannel shirts and blue jeans.

Leather and denim became part of a more flamboyant style for some men.

Designers exploited classic military tailoring to create outfits for the independent woman. This high-necked khaki jacket (1978) is offset with vampish makeup.

WOMEN'S MOVEMENT

In 1971, Germaine Greer's book *The Female Eunuch* urged women to free themselves from men and male values. Across the Western world, women burned their bras and stopped dressing to please men. The strict rules of fashion and beauty seemed outdated. The 1970s became a decade in which women fought for equal pay. To be successful, women felt they had to abandon traditional ideals of feminine fashion. The decade ended with a woman as prime minister in Britain.

Richard Roundtree became a style icon as the supercool star of the 1971 movie Shaft.

SERIOUS CLOTHES

Whether an individual was fighting for the cause of blacks, gays, or feminists, each became associated with a specific form of dress — a particular uniform. People could

BLACK PANTHERS

The Black Panther party, formed in 1966, was active throughout the 1970s. It fought for the rights of African-Americans. Black pride was a significant force in the 1970s. The Afro hairstyle, in particular, symbolized black culture.

Black leather jackets and black berets became the revolutionary fashion statement for many people.

Russian military styling had an air of icy, moody chic.

clearly show the views they held by the clothes they wore. By selecting clothes that were not fashionable — and, therefore, not subject to constant change — people were able to indicate the serious and permanent nature of their causes. Clothes had become a form of silent communication. Of course, anti-fashion soon became a fashion in its own right.

Denim for Everyone

In the 1850s, Levi Strauss began making tough work pants from denim, a cotton fabric consisting of white and blue threads. Originally, American gold miners wore these pants. By World War II, however, denim jeans had become work clothing for many people. The 1950s saw teenagers adopting jeans as their own. In the 1960s, jeans were transformed into frayed and embroidered flares. By the 1970s, denim appealed to just about everyone.

THE FIRST JEANS

Denim originated in the French town of Nîmes, for which the fabric was named. Tailor Levi Strauss had first used canvas to make hard-wearing pants, but then he came up with the idea of using dyed denim, instead. By 1873, he had patented a version of denim pants that incorporated copper rivets for extra strength.

California gold prospectors in the 1850s were the first to wear denim Levi's.

JEANS FOR ALL

In a decade when there were more fashions than ever from which to choose, jeans became a uniform. Because there were so many styles of jeans, they could be worn as part of any look.

FASHION STATEMENT

For some people, jeans were ultra-fashionable. Others chose them for their timeless appeal. Blue jeans were a way to avoid the frivolity of fashion. By the early 1970s, the feminist in jeans and the war protester in frayed flares were stereotypes.

For comfortable, day-to-day wear, colorful knit sweaters were worn with turned-up jeans.

Denim was not restricted to jeans. Denim vests, short jackets, and full-length coats also became popular.

Denim was the perfect uniform for rock concert fans around the world — and still is today!

CUSTOMIZED JEANS

People customized their jeans to suit their own styles. In 1973, recognizing the popularity of customizing jeans, Levi's held a Denim Art Contest. Hippies embroidered and patched their jeans. Glam rockers stitched their jeans with sequins. Punks ripped, pinned, and slashed their jeans. Disco queens wore theirs skin-tight with high heels and fluorescent socks. Whatever the look, jeans fit in.

JEANS FOR GROWN-UPS

Denim gained a respectability that reflected the increasing importance of casual, informal dress. Men and women combined Levi's with button-down shirts, sweaters, and loafers for a relaxed, unisex look. Jeans had become a classic.

Denim or no denim, Western boots and cowboy hats were popular.

DESIGNER DENIM

Designer jeans made their first appearance in the 1970s. In 1978, fifteen-year-old Brooke Shields modeled Calvin Klein's refitted, well-cut jeans. Two hundred thousand pairs were sold in the first week of the advertising campaign. Pierre Cardin (*b.* 1922), Ralph Lauren (*b.* 1939), and Elio Fiorucci (*b.* 1935) also designed denims.

DENIM ... EVERYWHERE!

More than just jeans were manufactured in denim. Everything that could be made in denim, was! The collection included traditional work shirts, hats, bags, bikinis, and shoes. Items such as car seats were also covered in denim. You could even buy a denim radio!

Overalls, worn with lace-up boots, provided practical fashion for both men and women.

Punk Fashion

Punk was born in Malcolm McLaren's and Vivienne Westwood's London clothing shop in 1975. McLaren asked a regular visitor to the shop, John Lydon, if he would join a band he was managing, called the Sex Pistols. Soon the band was making headlines with its bad behavior on stage and in public.

Do-it-yourself piercing became a punk stereotype.

REBEL WEAR

McLaren and Westwood opened their shop, first called "Let it Rock," at 430 Kings Road, in 1972. They sold copies of "teddy-boy" drape suits, the uniform of young rebels in the 1950s. By 1975, the shop was selling black rubber and leather wear and was a mecca for young punks.

NO FUTURE

In the mid-1970s, Britain was a depressing place for teenagers. With high unemployment, they felt they had no hope and no future. Even their music seemed stale and pointless. Teeny boppers and dressed-up glam rockers had nothing to say about real life.

Punk hair was dyed in Day-Glo colors — yellow, green, blue, orange, or red. Many punks stiffened their hair with generous amounts of hair spray or gel to keep it in place.

Some people felt that members of the Sex Pistols band could not play or sing. Malcolm McLaren claimed he formed the group only to sell more pants.

The black leather jacket has been a symbol of youth rebellion since the 1940s. Punks added chains, studs, badges, safety pins, and paint to make it their own.

AMERICAN PUNK

Aggressive and shocking, punk music and fashion captured the anger and frustration felt by many teenagers. Punk styles flourished in the United States, although more subtly, perhaps, than in Britain. American punk was never as popular as British punk, yet its influence was crucial. When McLaren visited New York in 1973 and met the punk band the New York Dolls, he was impressed by reactions to their outrageous outfits.

DO-IT-YOURSELF

Punks used anti-fashion to express disgust at the aspirations of the middle class. They adopted clothing that was deliberately shocking and, often, physically repellent. Pushing safety pins through cheeks, ears, and every available area of clothing, they assaulted all notions of good taste. Punks flaunted many outrageous fashions in the streets. Suits and school uniforms were ripped and worn with outlandish makeup and hair to parody respectability. Their do-it-yourself look communicated rebellion.

PUNK CHIC

Although punk shocked the mainstream, it soon became an influence on mainstream fashion. By 1976, Italian *Vogue* was featuring pages of black clothing worn with aggressive accessories. In 1977, Zandra Rhodes unveiled her Punk Chic collection. The main difference was that her safety pins and embroidery were gold!

Zandra Rhodes created designer styles for punks.

The New Romantics

More than even high heels, feathers, ruffles, and satin, the key to the new romantic's look was the careful pose!

New romanticism was considered a style phenomenon of the early 1980s, when it was popularized by bands such as Adam and the Ants and Duran Duran. It actually began in the mid-1970s, but the term was not invented by the media until the beginning of the 1980s.

Formed in 1977, Adam and the Ants had a shaky start, until singer Adam Ant hired Malcolm McLaren as his style guru. In 1981, McLaren dressed the band as pirates, as "dandy" highwaymen, and as Prince Charming fairy-tale characters.

EARLY DAYS

The new romantics had punk roots but took more interest in clothes, posing, and nightclubbing than in anarchy, spitting, and sweaty dancing. When punk made headlines and chaos reigned, the new romantics went into hiding. Then, in 1978, when punk was dying, they reemerged in a London nightclub called Gossips, at "Bowie Night." By holding "Bowie Night" on a Tuesday, the club successfully excluded unfashionable weekend nightclubbers.

Hats, including the military beret and the 1940s-inspired pillbox, made a comeback with new romantic nightclubbers.

WAY-OUT COSTUMES

Art students and Bowie fans indulged in the retro dressing and futurism that had already marked other 1970s styles — but they went farther. Their style was theatrical, exotic, or historical. The most extreme transformed themselves into pirates, space captains, and Asian princesses.

WHAT'S IN A NAME?

"Romance" was frilled shirts, bows, floppy haircuts, and velvet knickers. "New" was the futuristic element that combined Bowie's Ziggy Stardust with the military styling of Roxy Music's ultracool front man, Bryan Ferry. New wave bands, such as Joy Division and Kraftwerk, gave the look a harder edge. They dressed in suits and ties or coveralls. When Malcolm McLaren's new shop PX opened in 1978, it catered to an industrial look before transforming into a romantic boutique. By the end of the 1970s, new romantics moved from the underground into the headlines.

Fashion house Chloé's 1977 interpretation of the romantic look featured a lace shirt and a cavalier hat.

THE NEW ROMANTIC SOUND

Initially, the new romantics listened to music by David Bowie, Roxy Music, and Kraftwerk. This futuristic sound seemed to be the perfect antidote to bubbly disco pop. Before long, the new romantics were creating pop music for themselves. Steve Strange and Visage, Boy George and Culture Club, and Adam and the Ants presented more visual effects than music. Videos promoted pop music and provided an opportunity to flaunt the look.

Theatrical makeup and outrageous costumes propelled Steve Strange to the top of the charts.

Japanese Fashion

One of the most unexpected influences of the 1970s came from Japan. The Japanese designers who emerged in that decade are now among the most respected leaders of the fashion world. Their radical and intellectual work has been exhibited in art galleries and museums and has been sold in shops across the globe.

Kansai Yamamoto created dramatic garments inspired by Japanese culture (1971).

Kenzo's cropped kimono top and sarong skirt (1976) featured his trademark bold prints.

KIMONOS AND OBIS

The first Japanese designer to make a name in Western fashion was Hanae Mori (*b.* 1926). She worked within Western traditions but based many of her designs on the traditional Japanese kimono — a loose, wide-sleeved robe fastened at the waist with a broad sash called an obi.

KABUKI THEATER FASHION

Kyoto-born Kenzo (*b.* 1940) sparked interest in Japanese fashion when he opened a shop in Paris in 1970. Although not as radical as those who followed, Kenzo did make a departure from fussy Parisian couture. His styles, often inspired by the bold designs of Kabuki theater, were fun. They demonstrated his impressive ability in layering patterns and prints.

This Kansai Yamamoto design has a jockey theme with numbers and jodhpurs. It is topped with a padded satin kimono.

SWATHES AND LAYERS

In his publication *East Meets West*, Issey Miyake (*b*. 1935) stated that Western clothes are shaped with the body as the starting point. He explained that the Japanese approach is completely different. Japanese designers start with the fabric, so the emphasis is on layers, textures, and patterns. In a decade that favored figure-hugging clothes, the most radical Japanese fashions appeared completely unwearable to Western eyes.

THE RADICAL GENERATION

As Japanese designers began executing their ideas more boldly, Issey Miyake combined Eastern materials and color schemes with state-of-the-art manufacturing techniques. For his first collection, in 1970, he showed jeans in quilted sashiko, a material traditionally used for judo and kendo, or fencing, clothes. Kansai Yamamoto (*b*. 1944) also used sashiko. In 1971, Yamamoto opened his own house of design, featuring a unique and abstract style, heavily influenced by Kabuki puppet theater. Tokyo-born Rei Kawakubo (*b*. 1942) formed the fashion company Comme des Garçons in 1969. She created voluminous garments that disregarded body shape and experimented with torn and tattered fabrics. All of these Japanese designers went on to be highly influential in the 1980s and slowly revolutionized Western attitudes toward fashion.

When unzipped, this dramatic cape by Yamamoto reveals a skin-tight playsuit with a matching Kabuki mask design.

The Technology of Fashion

The most popular fabrics of the 1970s reflect the number of contrasting styles of the time. From the old to the new, the natural to the synthetic, almost every fabric and technique found favor for its own specific qualities.

Fake fur, made of acrylic and nylon, allowed for glamour without cruelty and a 1940s film-star look.

BACK TO BASICS

Not all designers sought high-tech methods. Bill Gibb was famous for his appliqué evening wear, to which ornamental pieces of fabric were sewn or glued. Zandra Rhodes explored every traditional means of producing and decorating fabric. Her designs were printed by hand, and her signature garments were quilted, embroidered, and sewn by hand.

NATURAL FABRICS

Popular fabrics included cheesecloth and denim. Most cheesecloth was imported from India, where it was embroidered and dyed by hand. Denim was mass-produced and was treated in various ways to achieve different effects. It was, for example, stonewashed with pumice to create a soft, faded look.

BUILT TO STRETCH

New technological developments in textile production were important for sportswear, day wear, and evening wear. Lycra, with its ability to stretch, keep its shape, and improve the drape of a garment, changed the face of fashion.

Zandra Rhodes models a tunic of her own design. Her textiles were inspired by everything from feathers to cacti and were all made painstakingly by hand.

Model Twiggy was a fan of Bill Gibb's romantically trimmed evening dresses.

in the 1970s

1
2
3

Lycra is always mixed with another fiber to give the resulting fabric maximum strength and stretch. Mixing the fibers also improves the fabric's feel and drape, or the way it hangs. Here (right), white strands of Lycra are interwoven with purple strands of cotton jersey.

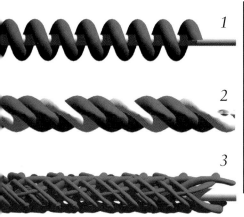

Lycra can be added to another fiber in different ways (above): it can be covered by another fiber (1); it can be twisted with another yarn as it is spun (2); or it can be forced through an air jet with another fiber, which coats it in a lacework of strands (3).

Introduced by Du Pont in 1958 as a trademarked type of spandex, Lycra was first used in swimwear, leotards, and underwear. Because it clings to the body, stretches, dries within minutes, and always keeps its shape, it was a practical fabric for the sportswear, dancewear, and disco fashions of the 1970s.

SLINKY SYNTHETICS

Synthetics and other manufactured fibers came into their own in the 1970s. Retro chic revisited fabrics of earlier decades, such as nylon, rayon, lamé, and Lurex. Glam and disco fashions exploited the slinky properties of synthetics. Lurex was a metallic thread that sparkled as it caught the light and was effective for evening wear. Rayon was a manufactured alternative to silk. In the 1970s, 1940s-style dresses were made in flower-printed rayon. Designers in the 1970s proved that the greater the selection of fabrics and technologies, the more wild and inventive fashion can become.

Lycra's stretchiness made it a perfect fabric for sportswear.

Lamé is a fabric containing metallic threads that glitter and shine. Clever weaving created patterns, such as these black and gold flowers (1976).

· T I M E   L I N E ·

	FASHION	WORLD EVENTS	TECHNOLOGY	FAMOUS PEOPLE	ART & MEDIA
1970	•*The name* hot pants *is coined by* Women's Wear Daily	•*U.S. troops sent into Cambodia* •*Chile: Allende elected president*	•*First video cassette recorders*	•*The Beatles split up*	•*Germaine Greer:* The Female Eunuch •*Andrew Lloyd Webber:* Jesus Christ Superstar
1971	•*French couturier Coco Chanel dies* •*Kansai Yamamoto opens his fashion house*	•*Uganda: Idi Amin seizes power* •*Indo-Pakistan war results in Bangladesh independence*	•*USSR launches first space station, Salyut 1* •*OMNIMAX cinema invented*	•*Muhammad Ali loses world heavy-weight title to Joe Frazier*	•*David Bowie:* Starman •*Ken Russell:* The Devils •*Stanley Kubrick:* A Clockwork Orange
1972	•*Bill Gibb opens his fashion house* •*Karl Lagerfeld:* "Deco" collection	•*SALT I treaty signed by U.S. and USSR* •*Britain imposes direct rule in Ulster*	•*First video games* •*First electronic calculator*	•*Bobby Fischer takes world chess title from Boris Spassky*	•*Tutankhamen exhibition in London* •*Francis Ford Coppola:* The Godfather
1973	•*Issey Miyake has his first show in Paris* •*Levi's holds its Denim Art Contest*	•*Yom Kippur War* •*OPEC oil price increases lead to economic crisis in West*	•*U.S. launches* Skylab *space station* •*Mountain bike invented*	•*Salvador Allende assassinated*	•*Jørn Utzon's Sydney Opera House completed*
1974	•*Jeff Banks launches Warehouse*	•*Turkey invades and occupies one-third of Cyprus*	•*First practical wave-powered generator*	•*U.S. President Nixon resigns over Watergate* •*Harold Wilson is British prime minister*	•*Fellini:* Amarcord •*ABBA:* Waterloo
1975	•*Punk style is born in McLaren's and Westwood's Kings Road shop*	•*End of Vietnam War* •*Cambodia overrun by Pol Pot's Khmer Rouge*	•*French company, BIC, invents disposable razors* •*First ultralight tested*	•*Spanish fascist dictator Franco dies; King Juan Carlos restored to throne*	•*Steven Spielberg:* Jaws •*Queen:* Bohemian Rhapsody
1976	•*Vivienne Westwood:* "Bondage" collection •*Yves Saint Laurent:* "Russian" collection	•*South Africa: Soweto riots result in more than 200 deaths*	•*U.S. Viking probes set down landers on Mars* •*The* Concorde's *first commercial flight*	•*China: Mao dies*	•*Christo:* Running Fence environmental sculpture •*Bob Marley:* Rastaman Vibration
1977	•*Zandra Rhodes:* "Punk Chic" collection •*Jean-Paul Gaultier starts his company*	•*UN bans arms sales to South Africa*	•*Apple II personal computer launched by Jobs and Wozniak* •*Speed sailing invented*	•*Steve Biko dies in South African police custody* •*Elvis Presley dies*	•*Derek Jarman:* Jubilee •*Sex Pistols:* God Save the Queen •*Paris: Pompidou Center completed*
1978	•*Brooke Shields models Calvin Klein's designer jeans*	•*Camp David peace treaty signed by Egypt and Israel*		•*First test-tube baby, Louise Brown, born* •*Golda Meir dies*	•*John Travolta:* Saturday Night Fever
1979	•*Norman Hartnell, dressmaker to Queen Elizabeth II, dies*	•*Iran: Khomeini comes to power* •*Uganda: Amin deposed*	•*Sony Walkman invented* •*Erno Rubic devises his cube puzzle*	•*Margaret Thatcher becomes Britain's first woman prime minister*	•*Frank Stella:* Kastura •*Woody Allen:* Manhattan

Glossary

army surplus: stocks of excess and leftover military clothing and equipment made available for sale to the public at low prices.

art deco: a design style popular in the 1920s and 1930s that featured angular lines, geometric shapes, and bold colors.

Black Panthers: a political organization of militant African-Americans that was particularly active in the 1960s and 1970s.

bodysuit: a stretchy, close-fitting, one-piece garment that covers the torso and, sometimes, the legs.

"capsule" wardrobe: a small collection of individual clothing items that can be interchanged and coordinated to create a variety of outfits and looks.

jumpsuit: a one-piece garment, consisting of trousers or shorts with an attached shirt or blouse.

Kabuki: a type of popular Japanese theater, dating back to the 1600s, that traditionally featured an all-male cast, colorful costumes and makeup, and exaggerated acting.

leg warmers: footless woolen socks that cover the lower leg, sometimes extending over the knee.

Lurex: the trade name of a shiny, metallic yarn or thread that is often interwoven or knitted with another fiber, such as rayon.

Oxford bags: baggy, cuffed trousers, worn in the 1920s and 1930s, that became a popular retro style in the 1970s.

sarong: a long strip of fabric that wraps around the body, waist- or chest-high, to form a skirt or a dress.

Ultrasuede: a synthetic fabric, made of polyester and polyurethane, that looks and feels like suede.

More Books to Read

Costume Since 1945: Couture, Street Style and Anti-Fashion. Deirdre Clancy (Drama Publishers)

Fashion Sourcebooks: the 1970s. Fashion Sourcebooks (series). John Peacock (Thames and Hudson)

Fashions of a Decade: The 1970s. Fashions of a Decade (series). Jacqueline Herald (Facts on File)

Great Fashion Designs of the Seventies: Paper Dolls in Full Color. Tom Tierney (Dover)

Haute Couture and Pret-A-Porter: Mode 1750–2000. Letse Meij, editor (Waanders Publishing)

Platform Shoes: A Big Step in Fashion. Ray Ellsworth (Schiffer)

Ralph Lauren, Master of Fashion. Wizards of Business (series). Anne Canadeo (Garrett Educational Corporation)

Streetstyle: From Sidewalk to Catwalk. Ted Polhemus (Thames and Hudson)

The Warhol Look. Mark Francis and Margery King, editors (Bulfinch Press)

Yves Saint Laurent. The Universe of Fashion (series). Pierre Berge and Grace Mirabella (Vendome Press)

Web Sites

Fashion Revues. Fashion: Chick and Slick. *www.xcentrix.com/Chic.htm*

Kingwood College Library: American Cultural History 1970-1979. (select: Fashion and Fads) *www.nhmccd.cc.tx.us/contracts/lrc/kc/decade70.html*

RETRO The Tip Tray. *www.retroactive.com/tiptray.html*

Timeline of Costume History. 20th Century Western Costume: 1970-1980 *www.costumes.org/pages/timelinepages/1970s1.htm*

Due to the dynamic nature of the Internet, some web sites stay current longer than others. To find additional web sites, use a reliable search engine with one or more of the following keywords: *anti-fashion, art deco, Cardin, denim, disco, embroidery, fur, Calvin Klein, Ralph Lauren, leotards, Lycra, preppie, punk, ready-to-wear, sportswear,* and *velour.*

Index